T3-BOC-375

25

THE FIRST TWENTY-FIVE YEARS

Commemorating its Silver Anniversary in 1985, ABC

Sports points with great pride to its role as the recognized

leader in sports television. The following pages celebrate

many of the remarkable moments and extraordinary

personalities that have woven a common thread through-

out the past two-and-a-half decades – 25 years of memo-

ries seen through the unique perspective of ABC Sports.

he 1960's were eye-opening and turbulent times, filled with mixed messages about the direction America was taking. Those were the years of Camelot in the Kennedy White House, but also a period of deep despair caused by the assassinations of JFK, his brother Bobby and Martin Luther King. There was the utter joy of the Beatles and Neil Armstrong's "giant step for mankind," as well as the horror of Vietnam and the effect it had on a generation of Americans. ■ ABC Sports was spawned during this landmark era in American history and, under the leadership of Roone Arledge, made its own unique mark by changing the face of sports television. ■ Prior to 1960, the ABC Television Network had no sports division as such. Sports Programs, Inc., headed by Edgar Scherick, independently produced the sporting events aired on ABC. That was to change drastically, however, as Scherick, ABC programming chief Tom Moore and a young man just hired from NBC by the name of Arledge, knew that a series of bold moves and calculated risks was the only way to put ABC Sports on the map. ■ In its first year of existence, ABC Sports gambled, but benefitted greatly, by securing the rights to the fledgling American Football League. In a major surprise, ABC also lured NCAA College Football from NBC – a move which elevated the network from virtual anonymity in sports coverage to a prestigious position in the battle for television supremacy. ■ It was September 11, 1960,

INTRODUCTION

when ABC Sports aired its first events – two regionally televised AFL contests featuring the Buffalo Bills at the New York Titans and the Houston Oilers at the Oakland Raiders. Just six days later, on September 17, college football made its ABC debut with Alabama vs. Georgia at Legion Field in Birmingham – a game which showcased a young Georgia quarterback named Fran Tarkenton. ■ History was made in yet another fashion during that Alabama-Georgia telecast as Arledge, producing the first of many events for ABC Sports, set out to cover sports as they never had been covered before. ■ As a prelude, he sent a detailed pre-game memo to his production staff, which included two other ABC Sports pioneers – Jim Spence, currently the Senior Vice President and Chuck Howard, now Vice President in Charge of Program Production. In that memorandum, Arledge simply set down certain guidelines that would be utilized on September 17. But, more importantly, they would serve to revolutionize sports coverage and distinguish ABC Sports from its competitors for many years to come. ■ The memo read, in part: *Television has done a remarkable job of bringing the game to the viewer – now we are going to take the viewer to the game. We will utilize every production technique that has been learned in producing variety shows, in covering political conventions, in shooting travel and adventure series, to enlighten the viewer's feeling of actually sitting in the stands and participating personally in the excitement and color of walking through a college campus to the stadium to watch the big game. All these delightful adornments to the actual contest have been missing from previously-televised sports events."* ■ That philosophy written by Arledge before the first college football telecast has been at the very heart of shaping ABC Sports and, in turn, the entire sports industry during the past quarter-century. Nowhere has it been as evident as on "ABC's Wide World of Sports." ■ In 1961, Moore and Scherick gave the go-ahead to formulate a new show on summer weekend afternoons. Created as a replacement series to continue the momentum college football had given the network, the concept of "Wide World of Sports" evolved and soon became an American institution – defying the odds by presenting events that had not yet received TV exposure. Arledge and Chuck Howard, then a production assistant, compiled a list of every sporting event scheduled and traveled the world purchasing the rights to the show's first year of programming. ■ Arledge's first coup was the acquisition of Amateur Athletic Union events, including the U.S.-U.S.S.R. Track and Field Meet in Moscow. Other competitions on "Wide World" during those early days were both the Penn and Drake Relays, which were the elements of the premiere telecast on April 29; the LeMans Grand Prix auto race from France; the F.A. Cup Soccer Championship from London; the Japanese All-Star Baseball game; World Championship Professional Tennis; and the Cheyenne Frontier Days Rodeo. ■ In need of a host for this kaleidoscope of events, Arledge displayed another stroke of genius by convincing CBS commentator Jim McKay to join the new series. Not only has McKay served with distinction in this role since the series' inception, but he has also become one of broadcasting's most respected and honored personalities. ■ *"'Wide World of Sports' was conceived as a showcase for the vast range of human endeavors we classify as sporting activities,"* explains Arledge, who can boast that the show has covered over 1000 events fitting into more than 120 different sports, from 47 states and 50 countries on six continents, during the past 25 years. *"We know that countless millions of people have followed sports that were not widely known in this country, perhaps not even played here in the U.S. Surely, if we could present these great spectacles to the American people in a meaningful way, we could provide attractive television entertainment, broaden the knowledge and perspective of the viewer, and maybe even make a contribution to understanding among the peoples of the world. Our philosophy throughout has been to focus on the people of sports, showing viewers who they are, what they are like, and why they have devoted so much of their lives to the pursuit of excellence…and we have tried to place our coverage of the spectacle of events in the context of their cultural, historic and geographic perspectives."* The "Wide World" gamble certainly proved that an audience could be created for sports for which no mass interest had been displayed before. It also has gone far in helping to popularize certain sports, such as gymnastics and figure skating. ■ These tenets, along with those designed for ABC's early college football coverage, have been at the foundation of "Wide World of Sports" programming from the start. The philosophies have carried into all other areas of ABC Sports as well – especially in the growth of its Olympic coverage, which has been called "the ultimate 'Wide World of Sports.'"

60's

ABC Sports was on its way to the top during the 1960's with its coverage of college football and "ABC's Wide World of Sports," which included major championship boxing highlighted by the frequent appearances of Cassius Clay (Muhammad Ali). ABC also reaped the benefits of gaining exclusive rights to a host of other outstanding series and single events. ■ In January of 1962, the "Professional Bowlers Tour" made its debut and is still going strong. "The American Sportsman" began in 1965 and was a network mainstay for 20 years. The Sixties also saw four prestigious golf tournaments begin long associations with ABC that still remain intact: the British Open in 1962, the PGA Championship in 1965 and the U.S. Open and U.S. Women's Open in 1966. ABC began a run of nine seasons of NBA basketball coverage with the 1964-65 season, and the Indianapolis "500," the world's greatest auto race, and the Gator Bowl made their first appearances on the network in 1965. ABC's first Olympics was telecast in 1964 with the Winter Games from Innsbruck, Austria. The newly-created ABC Olympic Tradition continued into the decade with the 1968 Winter Games from Grenoble, France and the '68 Summer Olympics from Mexico City. ■ In addition

THE SIXTIES

to programming, ABC Sports boasted a stable of outstanding announcers, such as Jim McKay, Howard Cosell, Chris Schenkel and Curt Gowdy, developed the expert commentator's role, and utilized the talents of Julius Barnathan and the ABC Engineering Department. ABC also was at the forefront of innovation during the 1960's with an impressive list of accomplishments that included: the first sports telecast from behind the Iron Curtain with the U.S.–U.S.S.R. Track and Field Meet from Moscow in 1961; the first use of the slow-motion instant replay technique in black and white (1961) and underwater cameras for swimming and diving (1962); the first live satellite coverage of the Olympics (Closing Ceremonies in Innsbruck, 1964); the first live sports telecast from the Soviet Union to the United States (U.S. – U.S.S.R. Track and Field Meet at Kiev in 1965); the first use of a 16:1 lens (longest focal lens of its time), at the 1966 Michigan State-Notre Dame NCAA football game; the first use of camera cranes in golf and other sports (1966 U.S. Open); the first usage of a variety of techniques in tape and effects: split screens, multiple screens, quadruple screens (1967); the first wireless hand-held broadcast color camera for closeups both with cable (1967) and without (1968); and the first color coverage of the Olympics, including slow-motion (Grenoble, 1968). ■ ABC Sports entered the decade as the new kid on the block – and ended it as the world leader

Top:
The history of ABC Sports began with AFL Football in
1960. Here, in 1962, ABC expert commentator Paul
Christman introduces the Houston Oilers, including
all-time greats Billy Cannon (20) and George Blanda
(16).

Center:
Later an NFL All-Pro and "Monday Night Football"
commentator, quarterback Fran Tarkenton made his
ABC debut in 1960, in the network's first college football telecast. The game featured Fran's Georgia Bull-
dogs vs. Coach Bear Bryant's Alabama Crimson Tide,
who won 21-6.

Bottom:
Jack Biondolillo in 1967, right before he cinched the
first perfect game on ABC's Pro Bowlers Tour.

Top:
Host Jim McKay, as he reported from the Penn Relays
in Philadelphia on the very first telecast of "ABC's Wide
World of Sports," April 29, 1961.

Center:
The series logo as it looked on the premiere show.

Bottom:
Roone Arledge and Chuck Howard map out their
scheduling plans for the next "Wide World" telecast.

History was made more than once on ABC Sports' coverage of U.S.–U.S.S.R. Track and Field Meets in the
1960's:
Top:
High jumper Valery Brumel broke through the Cold
War and became an American hero with his world
record jump at Moscow in 1961–the highlight of the
first sports telecast from behind the Iron Curtain.

Center:
Soviet leaders Leonid Brezhnev (far left) and Nikita
Khrushchev (third from left) and U.S. diplomat Averell
Harriman (far right) look on at Moscow's Lenin Stadium
in 1963 as Brumel once again broke a world record in
front of ABC cameras.

Bottom:
Bill Flemming, who reported from the Drake Relays on
the first "Wide World of Sports" telecast, anchors ABC's
control point in Rome during the network's coverage
of the meet from Kiev in 1965–the first live sports
telecast from the Soviet Union to the United States.

  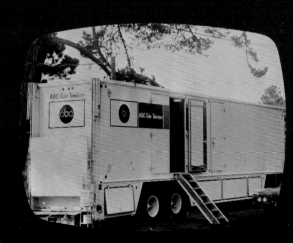

Top:
Speedskater Terry McDermott was the only U.S. gold medalist when ABC televised its first Olympics—the 1964 Winter Games from Innsbruck, Austria.

Center:
U.S. ski coach Bob Beattie, who later became an ABC Sports commentator, is flanked by Billy Kidd (left) and Jimmy Heuga (right), who won the first-ever U.S. medals in men's alpine skiing with a silver and bronze, respectively, in the slalom at Innsbruck in 1964.

Bottom:
ABC's Chris Schenkel (left) and Dick Button interview 1968 Olympic gold medalist Peggy Fleming. Button and Fleming later became colleagues on ABC figure skating telecasts.

Top:
USC's O.J. Simpson, now a member of the ABC Sports family, was college football's dominant player in the late 1960's—winning the Heisman Trophy in 1968. His last regular season game, vs. UCLA, was seen on ABC.

Center:
Baseball legends Leo Durocher and Jackie Robinson were commentators for ABC Sports' coverage of the national pastime in the 1960's.

Bottom:
Now a well-respected member of the ABC golf announcing crew, Dave Marr won the prestigious PGA tournament in 1965—the first year ABC Sports aired the event.

Top:
Howard Cosell, closely identified with ABC Sports boxing coverage over the years, was the foremost chronicler of the career of Muhammad Ali. He also was Ali's staunchest defender when the controversial fighter refused to be inducted into the Army because of his religious beliefs—and ultimately was stripped of his title.

Center:
ABC Sports covered Wimbledon in 1963 when Chuck McKinley won the men's singles title.

Bottom:
During the 1960's, ABC Sports control trucks were becoming a common sight at major sporting events everywhere.

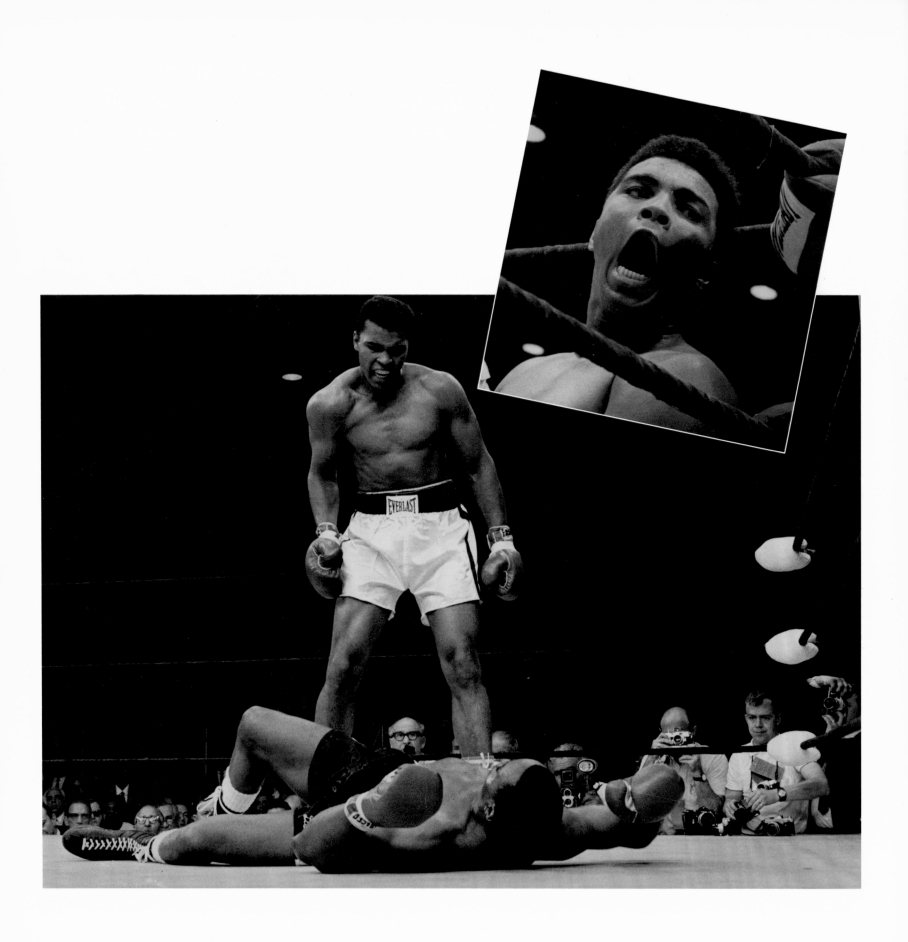

These are the Opening Ceremonies at the 1964 Winter Olympics in Innsbruck, Austria – the beginning of ABC Sports' Olympic Tradition. Since then, ABC has distinguished itself by also presenting Winter Games from Grenoble (1968), Innsbruck (again in 1976), Lake Placid (1980) and Sarajevo (1984), and Summer Olympics from Mexico City (1968), Munich (1972), Montreal (1976) and Los Angeles (1984). □ In 1988, ABC Sports will present its tenth Olympics – the XV Winter Olympic Games from Calgary.

The epitome of beauty and grace, Peggy Fleming reached the pinnacle of her remarkable figure skating career by winning the only U.S. gold medal at the 1968 Winter Olympics. ☐ It was altogether appropriate that ABC Sports was there to cover her greatest success, because "Wide World of Sports" was instrumental in introducing Peggy to the public–including coverage of all five of her national titles. She came full circle in 1981 by joining the ABC Sports team as a figure skating analyst.

f one athlete was identified with ABC Sports and mirrored the network's rise to the top in the 1960's, it was Muhammad Ali —who began the decade as Cassius Clay. □ Brashly proclaiming, "I am the greatest," the enormously-skilled boxer became a familiar sight to viewers of ABC Sports. Ali's first appearances on ABC were his shocking seventh-round TKO of Sonny Liston for the heavyweight crown in 1964 at Miami Beach and his first title defense (1965) when he retained the championship by flooring, and then taunting, Liston in a first round KO at Lewiston, Maine.

Jim Beatty will always hold a special place in the sports record books – as the first to run the sub-four minute mile indoors. "ABC's Wide World of Sports" was on hand when Beatty accomplished the feat, running a remarkable 3:58.09 at the Los Angeles Times Meet in February of 1962. □ By virtue of his history-making accomplishment, Beatty also earned the distinction of being named the first "Wide World of Sports Athlete of the Year." Subsequently, the honor has been bestowed on all of the following, a "Who's Who" of the world's premier athletes: Valery Brumel, Don Schollander, Jim Clark, Jim Ryun, Peggy Fleming, Bill Toomey, Mario Andretti, Willis Reed, Lee Trevino, Olga Korbut, O.J. Simpson, Jackie Stewart, Muhammad Ali, Jack Nicklaus, Nadia Comaneci, Steve Cauthen, Ron Guidry, Willie Stargell, the 1980 U.S. Olympic Hockey Team, Sugar Ray Leonard, Wayne Gretzky, the crew of Australia II and Edwin Moses.

As the host of "ABC's Wide World of Sports" since the very first telecast, Jim McKay has traveled the world covering virtually every sport imaginable. He is shown here at various events during the 1960's, living up to the "Wide World" motto: "Spanning the globe to bring you the constant variety of sport ... the thrill of victory, the agony of defeat, the human drama of athletic competition."

Almost two years before the premiere of ABC Sports'"The American Sportsman," an event aired on "Wide World of Sports" in May of 1963 which led to the creation of the long-running, award-winning series—a trout fishing expedition to Lago General Paz, Argentina, along the Chilean border. This, however, was not simply a fishing trip. It was a contest for the "World Trout Fishing Championship." Sportscaster Curt Gowdy (far right), later the host of "American Sportsman," and fishing legend Joe Brooks (second from right) competed against two wealthy Argentine ranchers (left)—each of whom was renowned for his fishing skills. Roone Arledge (center), then Executive Producer of ABC Sports, liked the idea so much he joined the expedition as a field producer as well as the referee/timekeeper.

Arnold Palmer was golf's premier superstar in the early 1960's, boosting the sport's prestige with his engaging and energetic personality – and his ability to win golf tournaments. Palmer and his fans, who became known as "Arnie's Army," represented one of the major sports stories of the decade. □ ABC Sports vividly brought the Palmer phenomenon to the public. ABC cameras were at the 1962 British Open in Troon, Scotland – the network's first coverage of the event – when Palmer won his second British title in a row. In 1966, when ABC covered its inaugural U.S. Open, at the Olympic Club in San Francisco, Palmer was again a central figure. Pictured here, Arnie – who led by seven strokes going into the final holes – shows his anguish after missing a putt for par at 17. Moments later, Billy Casper tied things up, sending them into an 18-hole playoff the next day. Even the masterful Palmer couldn't pull it out, as Casper won the playoff in dramatic fashion. □ A historic footnote to this memorable tournament is that Arnie would never again win a major championship.

With ABC Sports' Bill Flemming on the scene, President Richard Nixon presents a plaque to University of Texas football coach Darrell Royal, proclaiming the Longhorns as the nation's No. 1 college football team in 1969. Nixon's controversial gesture came immediately after Texas scored a thrilling, 15-14, victory over archrival Arkansas.

One of the great skiers of all time, Jean-Claude Killy thrilled ABC audiences with three gold medal performances at the 1968 Winter Games in Grenoble. He was victorious in the downhill, slalom and giant slalom at these Olympics, held in his native France.

Reflecting their country's racial unrest, U.S. Olympians Tommie Smith (center) and John Carlos (right) caused a major controversy at the 1968 Summer Olympics with their black-gloved, clenched fist "Black Power Salute," following their gold and bronze medal performances in the 200-meter dash. □ Super-heavyweight George Foreman (inset), who years later would become the heavyweight champion of the world in the pro ranks, followed his own convictions in the wake of the Smith-Carlos protest. After his gold medal victory, Foreman walked around the ring waving an American flag, endearing him to the crowd at ringside in Mexico City as well as to millions of ABC viewers watching at home.

Bill Toomey (right), despite bad health and a withered hand, followed in the tradition of U.S. decathlon champions Jim Thorpe, Bob Mathias and Rafer Johnson, as he won the gold medal in the grueling two-day, ten event competition at the 1968 Olympics in Mexico City. Here, he battles East Germany's Manfred Tiedtke in the 110-meter hurdles.

mid the racial controversy of the Mexico City Olympics, long jumper Bob Beamon set one of the most remarkable records in the history of sports. With a jump of 29 feet, 2½ inches, he broke the existing record by an amazing 16 inches – an increase in distance unparalleled in track history. □ Following his gold medal jump, Beamon had this to say to those offering congratulations – "Tell me I'm not dreaming."

The picture tells the story as car owner Andy Granatelli plants a kiss on the cheek of Mario Andretti in "victory lane," after Mario drove to his first Indianapolis "500" triumph (1969).

70's

In just one decade, ABC Sports climbed to the summit of network sports television. And, as was the case ten years before with college football and "Wide World of Sports," ABC took a bold, new step as the 1970's began—with the introduction of a pro football series in prime time. ■ ABC's NFL "Monday Night Football," whose announcers became bigger celebrities than the players themselves, finally gave Americans a reason to look forward to Mondays. The series became one of television's top attractions and set the tone for an innovative and action-packed decade for ABC Sports. There also were ABC's first telecast of the Sugar Bowl (1970); rights to the first two jewels of thoroughbred racing's Triple Crown with the Kentucky Derby (1975) and Preakness Stakes (1977); the network's first long-term Major League Baseball package (1976) including the League Championship Series ('76) and the World Series (1977); and a continuation of the most prestigious professional and amateur boxing matches on TV, including the classic confrontations between Muhammad Ali and Joe Frazier. ■ It was during the 1970's, too, that ABC began earning the distinction of the "Network of the Olympics," providing coverage of its fourth, fifth and sixth Games—the

THE SEVENTIES

1972 Summer Olympics from Munich and both the 1976 Winter and Summer Games, from Innsbruck and Montreal, respectively. ■ ABC Sports also continued to be at the forefront of innovation. During the decade of the 70's, ABC pioneered the use of multiple end zone and isolation cameras in football, combining two basic pickup units, one for game action and the other for analysis (1971); televised the table tennis matches between the United States and the People's Republic of China in 1971 from China—the first sports competition between the two countries—and in 1972 aired the historic rematch as the Chinese athletes traveled to the U.S. (Detroit, Michigan); introduced the "Up Close and Personal," an innovation closely identified with ABC Sports' Olympics coverage, which was born out of the network's philosophy of focusing on the people in sports (1972 Summer Olympics, Munich); showed the first downhill ski race from top to bottom (1976 Winter Olympics, Innsbruck); was the first to use a 3,000 meter zoom lens (Innsbruck, 1976); and became the first to utilize what turned out to be the largest mobile unit in the world (40-foot vans with eight cameras, two tape machines, three slow-motion devices plus character generators, 24 video units and 34 audio inputs) (1976). ■ For ABC Sports, the decade of the 1970's was an era to continue the great progress that began in the 1960's—and to lead the way as the golden age of sports television flourished.

NFL MONDAY NIGHT FOOTBALL

The phenomenon of ABC's NFL "Monday Night Football"...

Top:
The graphic opening on the first telecast, September 21, 1970.

Center:
Roone Arledge and commentators Don Meredith, Howard Cosell and Keith Jackson before the first game in the series' history – Joe Namath and the New York Jets vs. the Browns in Cleveland.

Bottom:
Chet Forte (left) has served as either the producer or director of "Monday Night Football" since its inception. Here, he takes a breather in the control truck with Dennis Lewin, who was a producer during the prime time series' first decade and is currently a Vice President and the Coordinating Producer of "Wide World of Sports."

Top, Center, Bottom:
Yugoslavian ski jumper Vinko Bogataj became an instant celebrity in the United States as a result of this 1970 spill at Oberstdorf, West Germany – and will be forever identified as the "Agony of Defeat" on "Wide World of Sports."

Top:
A somber Jim McKay tells American viewers the tragic news that Arab terrorists have killed 11 Israeli Olympic Team members during the 1972 Summer Games in Munich.

Center:
Between 1970 and 1977, 300+ pound Soviet weight-lifter Vassily Alexeyev set 80 world records and awed ABC viewers by winning Olympic gold medals at both Munich and Montreal.

Bottom:
U.S. basketball players Dwight Jones (left) and Mike Bantom sit in disbelief as the United States has just been defeated, 51-50, by the Soviet Union in the gold medal game at the 1972 Summer Olympics. In one of the most controversial finishes ever, the U.S. suffered its first loss in Olympic play – snapping a 62-game victory streak.

Top:
ABC Sports covered the North American Soccer League in the 1970's and 1980's, as well as presenting the great Pele's (left) tearful farewell performance as a New York Cosmo in 1977.

Center:
ABC frequently reported on the exploits of daredevil Evel Knievel, including his much-publicized 1974 attempt to jump the Snake River Canyon in Idaho.

Bottom:
Kurt Thomas was America's premier gymnast in the late 1970's and in 1978 became the first American to win a world title in gymnastics–a feat documented by "Wide World of Sports."

Top:
Colorful golfer Lee Trevino won four major titles on ABC in the 1970's–the '71 U.S. Open, '71-'72 British Opens and '74 PGA–and has claimed six on the network in all.

Center:
Bob Uecker, Warner Wolf and Bob Prince were the primary announcers when ABC Sports began covering baseball again in 1976.

Bottom:
Sugar Ray Leonard (above) was one of five U.S. Olympic boxing gold medalists at Montreal in 1976. The others were Michael and Leon Spinks, Leo Randolph and Howard Davis. The Spinks twosome later became the only brother combination to hold world heavyweight titles and the others, except for Davis, won professional championships as well.

Top:
Bill Russell and Keith Jackson called the action on ABC Sports' NBA telecasts.

Center:
ABC's "Superstars" was one of TV's most popular sports series in the 1970's and 1980's, featuring the world's greatest athletes performing in sports other than their specialties.

Bottom:
Quarterback Archie Manning led Mississippi to a 27-22 victory over Arkansas on ABC's first Sugar Bowl telecast, in 1970.

Beginning in 1970, "Monday Night Football" established itself as a television institution, with its announcers achieving the same celebrity status as other prime time personalities. Howard Cosell, Don Meredith and Frank Gifford shared the booth for the longest time (ten years) while such familiar names as Keith Jackson, Alex Karras, Fran Tarkenton and most recently, O.J. Simpson and Joe Namath, also have contributed to the enormous success of the series.

In a 1970's cause celebre televised by ABC Sports, tennis great Billie Jean King is carried in on a throne, moments before her much-ballyhooed 1973 "Battle of the Sexes" match with hustler Bobby Riggs at Houston's Astrodome. A former tennis champion and self-proclaimed "male chauvinist pig," Riggs proved to be no match for Ms. King, who won in straight sets. Although the event was a light-hearted one, it represented a pivotal point for the equality of women in sports.

n 1970, ABC Sports covered one of the truly great championship series in NBA history – highlighted by the courageous performance of Willis Reed (shown here shooting over Wilt Chamberlain) as he led the New York Knicks over the Los Angeles Lakers for their first league title. ☐ Reed, injured in the fifth game, wasn't expected to play in the deciding seventh game in New York. But moments before the start of the contest, he appeared on the court ready to go – winning the approval of the jubilant hometown fans. Despite being in considerable pain, Reed scored the first two baskets, setting the tone for the Knicks victory and establishing himself as the series MVP.

Muhammad Ali, the only box-er to hold the heavyweight title three times, won the crown for the second time in this convincing eighth round knockout of George Foreman at Kinshasa, Zaire, in 1974. ABC Sports cameras were also on hand in 1978 when Ali claimed the championship for the third time—against Leon Spinks in New Orleans.

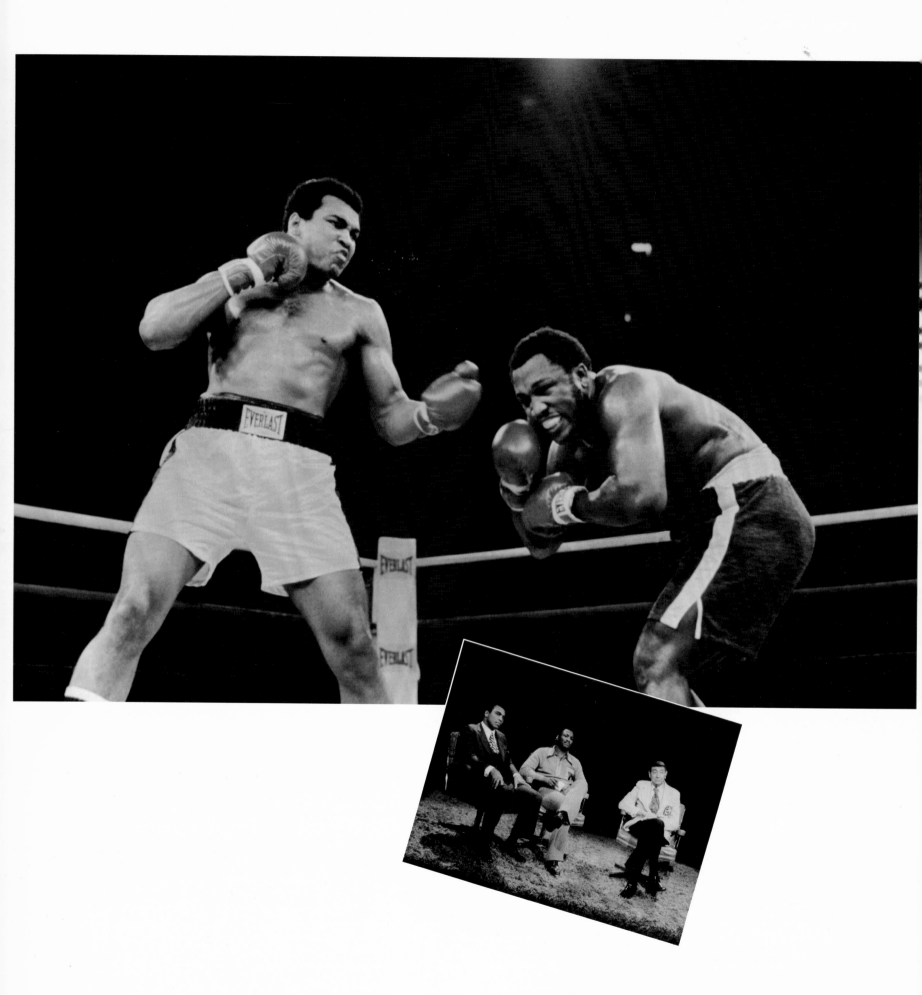

ABC Sports televised all three of the classic battles between Muhammad Ali and Joe Frazier in the 1970's. □ Frazier won the first bout, successfully defending his heavyweight crown with a 15-round decision at New York's Madison Square Garden in 1971. Ali got revenge at the Garden in 1974, with a 12-round decision in a non-title fight, and then, in 1975, retained his title (won the year before against George Foreman) with a 14th round TKO of Frazier in the "Thrilla in Manila." □ Howard Cosell interviewed both Ali and Frazier (inset) on "Wide World of Sports" shortly before their second fight. Moments after this scene, the two fighters wound up in a spontaneous brawl after Ali called Frazier "ignorant."

he darling of the 1976 Innsbruck Olympics was figure skater Dorothy Hamill. Her energetic style captured the hearts of ABC viewers back in the States, and her hairdo – the Hamill Cut – became a national sensation.

One of the most exciting moments in ABC Sports' Olympic history was Franz Klammer's breathtaking gold medal victory in the downhill at Innsbruck in 1976. □ The 22-year-old Klammer, with the pressure of being the favorite in his native land, needed the run of his life to surpass the pacesetter, Bernhard Russi of Switzerland. He rose to the occasion with this super-human effort to edge Russi by one-third of a second.

Swimmer Mark Spitz established himself as one of the greatest Olympic athletes ever, with his record seven gold medals in 1972 at Munich. □ ABC viewers saw Spitz capture the gold in the 100 and 200 meter freestyles; 100 and 200 meter butterflys; 4 x 100 meter freestyle relay; 4 x 200 freestyle relay; and 4 x 100 meter medley relay.

Dave Wottle, the man with the familiar golf cap, emerged as one of the American heroes at the 1972 Munich Olympics with a thrilling come-from-behind victory in the 800 meters. □ Here is the "golden" moment for Wottle. He lunges toward the finish line to nip the favored Yevgeny Arzhanov (lower right corner) of the Soviet Union, who fell to the ground two meters short of the tape.

Throughout the 1960's and early 1970's ABC Sports covered the career of Jim Ryun—perhaps the greatest middle distance runner of all time. □ Despite his world records and Olympic silver medal, Ryun failed three times—1964, 1968, 1972—in his effort to win the Olympic gold. □ Here, at the '72 Games, Ryun (right) sees his hopes for gold dashed for good as he was tripped in his 1500-meter heat and did not qualify for the finals.

One of the heartwarming moments of ABC Sports' coverage of the 1976 Montreal Olympics – Edwin Moses (left) and Mike Shine embrace after winning the gold and silver medals, respectively, in the 400-meter hurdles. □ Moses, of course, went on to win another gold medal at the 1984 Games in Los Angeles,which gave him a consecutive streak of 105 victories dating back to 1977.

oncentrat

Exhilarat

had all of these qualitie

the 1976 Olympic de

at Montreal giving

A pair of diminutive teenage gymnasts from behind the Iron Curtain – Olga Korbut of the Soviet Union (opposite page) and Nadia Comaneci of Rumania – captivated American viewers during the two Summer Olympics of the 1970's. Due in large part to ABC's dedicated coverage of the sport, these two exceptional athletes came into prominence – and were ultimately responsible for the decade's boom in gymnastics popularity. □ Olga's skills won her three gold medals and a silver in 1972 at Munich, but it was her charm that won this 17-year-old pixie the hearts of Americans. □ In 1976 at Montreal, Nadia captured three golds, including the All-Around, a silver and a bronze. The 14-year-old marvel also received the first perfect scores of ten in Olympic history for her performances on the balance beam and uneven parallel bars – finishing the Games with an incredible seven perfect marks.

The classic rivalry between Affirmed and Alydar was the talk of horse racing in 1978 and ranks among the great thoroughbred confrontations of all time. ABC Sports was there to cover their down-to-the-wire battles in both the Kentucky Derby (shown here, with Affirmed in the lead on the right) and Preakness Stakes. □ In other years Alydar could have been a Triple Crown winner, but he had to settle for second in all three races to the brilliant Affirmed – who was jockeyed to glory by 16-year-old apprentice Steve Cauthen (inset).

ABC Sports' first telecasts of the League Championship Series and World Series couldn't have been filled with more drama. □ In 1976, the New York Yankees' Chris Chambliss (top photo, center) jumped for joy after powering a home run over the right field wall in the ninth inning of the fifth and deciding game of the American League Championship Series against Kansas City. It sent the Yanks into the World Series for the first time since 1964. □ In 1977, during ABC's first coverage of the fall classic, "Mr. October," Reggie Jackson (bottom photo), stole the show – slamming five home runs with 25 total bases in the Yankees' four games to two victory over the Los Angeles Dodgers. □ In Game 6, Reggie became the only player in Series history to hit three consecutive home runs in one game.

A new wave of patriotism hit the land as the 1980's began. ABC Sports mirrored America's mood as it began the decade with the excitement and national pride generated by the XIII Winter Olympic Games from Lake Placid, N.Y. – illuminated by the stunning gold medal victory by the U.S. Hockey Team and the five gold medal performance by speedskater Eric Heiden. Four years later, the American spirit reached its zenith as ABC covered the U.S. Olympic success in Sarajevo, Yugoslavia, and then took part in the remarkable phenomenon known as the Games of the XXIIIrd Olympiad in Los Angeles – the most memorable Olympics ever. ■ The 80's also have proven to be a landmark decade for ABC's football coverage with "Monday Night Football" now well into its second decade and ABC's telecast of its first Super Bowl – the most watched sporting event of all time – during the network's 25th anniversary year in 1985. Added to that ABC Sports began covering the powerhouse College Football Association in 1984, featuring the most attractive matchups in the college game. ■ Other key moments for ABC Sports in the first half of the 1980's included the 1981 premiere of Howard Cosell's "ABC SportsBeat"; the exclusive rights to cover the New York City Marathon, the largest U.S. marathon in terms of both participants and spectators, beginning in

THE EIGHTIES

'81; the coverage of the inaugural season of the innovative United States Football League (1983); and a greater emphasis on emerging new endurance events like the "Ironman Triathlon" and a cross-country cycling competition called "Race Across America." ■ Among the technical innovations introduced during the '80's have been: the reverse angle camera on "Monday Night Football" (1983); the first live microwave signal from the summit of Mt. Everest (1983); the use of vehicles capable of propelling themselves for as long as two-and-one-half hours, supporting heavy cameras, microphones, and power supplies for telecasting sporting events – without emitting gasoline fumes, which can affect athletes' performances (1983); the "super slo-mo" camera, giving a greater degree of clarity on slow-motion replays (1984); and the micro miniature camera, placed on the umpire's mask for a new perspective in baseball coverage (1985), and on a helmet worn by marathoner Rod Dixon as he ran portions of the '85 New York City Marathon. ■ Looking ahead to 1986, ABC Sports will present first-ever live network coverage of the Indianapolis "500" and will celebrate the Silver Anniversary of ABC's "Wide World of Sports." Then, in 1988, ABC Sports will present exclusive coverage of the XV Winter Olympic Games from Calgary, Canada – which will give ABC the

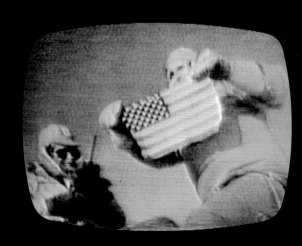

Top:
In 1982, Gordon Johncock and Rick Mears treated ABC viewers to the closest Indianapolis "500" finish in history. Johncock won by .16 of a second.

Center:
ABC Sports Senior Vice President Jim Spence (right) and Joseph Cloutier, Sr., President of the Indianapolis Motor Speedway, are shown at a 1985 press conference announcing the historic agreement for the first live network telecast of the Indianapolis "500" in 1986.

Bottom:
Joe Namath, who played in the first "Monday Night Football" telecast, joined Frank Gifford and O.J. Simpson in the broadcast booth in 1985 — giving the series an all-Hall of Fame crew.

Three memorable moments on "ABC's Wide World of Sports" during the 1980's:

Top:
Julie Moss, who collapsed and was passed just 10 yards away from the finish line, struggled courageously to finish second in the 1981 "Ironman Triathlon."

Center:
The team from Kirkland, Washington, led by Cody Webster (center, without cap), broke a six-year Far East dominance by defeating Pu-Tzu Town of the Republic of China (Taiwan), 6-0, in 1982 to win the Little League World Series — an event "Wide World" has aired for 23 straight years through 1985.

Bottom:
The Harlem Globetrotters, who have been a staple on the series since 1973, perform here with the famed Rockettes at New York's Radio City Music Hall for a 1983 telecast.

Top:
Howard Cosell interviews President Ronald Reagan for "ABC SportsBeat."

Center:
ABC Sportscaster Jack Whitaker talks to one of the sports world's biggest stars — golfer Jack Nicklaus.

Bottom:
In 1983, "The American Sportsman" delivered the first microwave signal from the summit of Mt. Everest.

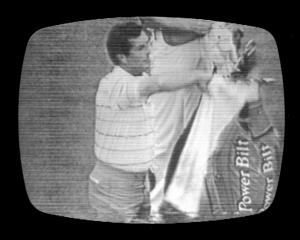

Top:
Chris Schenkel (right) and Nelson Burton, Jr. call the action for the "Pro Bowlers Tour" — one of the most popular sports series on television.

Center:
ABC beautifully captured the emotions of ice skater Irina Rodnina, as tears of joy rolled down her cheek after she and her husband, Alexander Zaitsev, won the gold in the pairs competition at the 1980 Winter Olympics in Lake Placid.

Bottom:
Julius Barnathan, President of ABC Broadcast Operations and Engineering, has been at the heart of ABC Sports' state-of-the-art technology.

Top:
Greco-Roman wrestler Jeff Blatnick breaks down during an interview with ABC Sports' Russ Hellickson after Blatnick, a victim of Hodgkins Disease, captured his gold medal at the 1984 Summer Olympics.

Center:
Frank Gifford embraces one of the competitors during ABC's coverage of the 1983 International Special Olympics.

Bottom:
Frank Broyles and Keith Jackson have teamed on ABC college football telecasts for nine seasons through 1985.

Top:
Versatile ABC Sportscaster Jim Lampley (right) is shown with 1984 Heisman Trophy winner Doug Flutie on the set of the CFA College Football studio show. Flutie joined ABC in 1985 after appearing as a player on the network's coverage of both college and USFL football.

Center:
ABC Sports cameras were there when Fuzzy Zoeller playfully signalled his surrender after Greg Norman sank a 45-foot putt on the 18th hole in the final round of regulation play at the 1984 U.S. Open. Norman returned the favor the following day when Zoeller clinched the victory in a playoff.

Bottom:
The moment it happened (on September 11, 1985), ABC Sportscaster Al Trautwig described the excitement of Pete Rose's 4,192nd hit — enabling the future Hall of Famer to surpass Ty Cobb and become the majors' all-time hit leader.

n 1983, the New York City Marathon provided ABC Sports viewers with one of the most exciting finishes in marathon history. □ Great Britain's Geoff Smith had a narrow lead over Rod Dixon of New Zealand in the final nine blocks of the race. But in the stretch, Dixon – inspired by the crowd – pulled away to win. Here, in this classic scene, the winner enjoys his triumph while the runnerup lies in agony.

Sugar Ray Leonard's charisma and boxing skills always invited comparison to Muhammad Ali. ☐ Like Ali's career, Leonard's fights were well-documented by ABC Sports, from his gold medal triumph in Montreal to his early pro career to his unforgettable title fights with Wilfred Benitez (1979), Roberto Duran (two in 1980) and Thomas Hearns (1981). ☐ Leonard's boxing career ended prematurely due to an eye injury in 1984, but not before he laid claim to both the World Welterweight and Junior Middleweight titles.

Perhaps the greatest golfer of all, Jack Nicklaus (opposite page) has treated ABC Sports viewers to countless standout performances – including ten major tournament victories. Here he is in 1980, during his record-tying fourth U.S. Open triumph, at Baltusrol. Nicklaus also won the PGA that year, at the age of 40. □ One of Jack's chief rivals over the years, Tom Watson hugs his caddy after winning the 1982 U.S. Open at Pebble Beach—a tournament in which he made a brilliant chip shot for a birdie on the 17th hole in the final round to break a tie with Nicklaus. Watson went on to birdie 18 and win his first Open championship by two strokes. □ In another memorable ABC-televised golf event, Watson and Nicklaus battled each other in the 1977 British Open, before Watson captured his second of five British titles.

n ABC Sports' first Super Bowl telecast (1985), Joe Montana, No. 16, led the super-charged San Francisco 49ers to an impressive, 38-16, victory over the Miami Dolphins in Palo Alto, California.

n 1960, the legendary Bear Bryant was the winning coach in ABC Sports' first college football telecast. □ In 1981, ABC was a witness to history, covering the Bear's 315th victory – a 28-17 Alabama win over archrival Auburn – making him the then-winningest college coach of all time. Bryant died in January of 1983, a month after coaching his final game.

Speedskater Eric Heiden made his mark as one of the truly great Olympic champions at the 1980 Winter Games in Lake Placid – winning an Olympic-record five individual gold medals.

Considered to be the greatest upset in the history of sports, the 1980 U.S. Olympic Hockey Team shocked the world with its 4-3 win over the Soviet Union. Later, the U.S. climaxed this "Miracle on Ice" by defeating Finland, 4-2, to win the coveted gold medal. □ The memories from ABC Sports' coverage of both games are etched in the minds of millions. Among them are the sight of goalie Jim Craig (left) searching for his widowed father after the gold medal victory and ABC Sportscaster Al Michaels' memorable call of the game against the Soviets. □ Michaels (below), best known as ABC's primary play-by-play announcer for Major League Baseball, will always be remembered for his six words, uttered as the seconds ticked off the clock ... "Do you believe in miracles? Yes!"

Although this may look like a two-photograph sequence of the same skier, it is really twin brothers Steve (left) and Phil Mahre on their way to winning silver and gold medals, respectively, in the slalom at the 1984 Winter Olympics in Sarajevo.

reat Britain's Jayne Torvill
and Christopher Dean
mesmerized viewers with their ice danc-
ing routines in Sarajevo and scored a
remarkable 12 perfect marks of 6.0.

ABC Sports cameras were right on the spot as the U.S. Team marched into the Los Angeles Coliseum during the Opening Ceremonies at the 1984 Summer Olympics. ☐ In the most-watched telecast in the history of television, more than two billion people—half the world's population—saw at least some part of ABC Sports' coverage. ABC broadcast 180 hours in 14 days and sent a world feed to 122 countries. Jim McKay (below), synonymous with the network's Olympic Tradition, hosted the prime time coverage in L.A.

arl Lewis was one of the U.S. heroes at the Los Angeles Games, equalling Jesse Owens' record feat of four track and field gold medals in one Olympics – in the 100- and 200-meter dashes, the long jump and 4 x 100 meter relay.

reg Louganis was poetry
in motion, winning gold
medals in both the platform and spring-
board diving events at Los Angeles.

In the most controversial incident of the
'84 Summer Games, World Champion
Mary Decker holds her left leg on the
sidelines after colliding with Zola Budd
in the 3,000 meter run – her gold medal
hopes gone.

ollowing in the footsteps of Olga Korbut and Nadia Comaneci, bundle of dynamite Mary Lou Retton had America in the palm of her hand at Los Angeles in 1984. She emerged as the world's premier female gymnast, winning the gold medal in the All-Around competition.

ABC Sports, in its first 25 years, has truly set the standard for sports television. With the ultimate in programming, on-air talent, producers, directors, other production and administrative personnel and the technological expertise of ABC's Broadcast Operations and Engineering department, the accomplishments of the "recognized leader in sports television" are just beginning. □ As Jim McKay so eloquently put it, "The Olympics of Los Angeles summed up everything we've been trying to do at ABC Sports for 25 years...To capture the thrill of victory and the agony of defeat, and also to explore the depths of human desire, determination and dedication. We'll move forward from here, to new events and new technology and new human drama." □ Nowhere will the new events, technology and human drama be more evident than during ABC Sports' exclusive coverage of the 1988 Winter Olympics in Calgary (inset).

ACKNOWLEDGMENTS

"ABC Sports: The First Twenty-Five Years" was written and developed by Art Berke, Manager, Sales Development, ABC Television Network.

Designer: Steve Hill, ABC Art Department; Photo Researcher: Pam Sztybel, ABC Visual Communication/Public Relations.

ABC Visual Communication/Public Relations provided the photographs for this book. All are ABC photographs with the exception of those supplied by the following sources: Wide World Photos; UPI/ Bettmann Newsphotos; Sports Illustrated; Ken Regan/Camera 5; The University of Georgia Sports Information Department; The XV Olympic Winter Games Organizing Committee; The Amateur Hockey Association of the United States; and Marcus Tullis.

ABC Sports expresses its thanks for the support of the management of American Broadcasting Companies, Inc., the ABC Broadcast Group – including the people of Broadcast Operations & Engineering, Business Analysis & Financial Planning, Public Relations, Program Administration, Marketing & Research Services – and the Sales, Affiliate Relations and Advertising & Promotion Departments of the ABC Television Network.

COPYRIGHT © 1985 AMERICAN BROADCASTING COMPANIES, INC.